DayOne

HELP!

I NEED TO KNOW ABOUT THE PROBLEMS OF ADOPTION

James Taylor

Consulting Editor: Dr. Jim Winter

© Day One Publications 2017
First printed 2017

ISBN 978-1-84625-570-0

All Scripture quotations, unless stated otherwise,
are from the New International Version 2011

Published by Day One Publications
Ryelands Road, Leominster, HR6 8NZ
Tel 01568 613 740   Fax 01568 611 473
North America Toll Free 888 329 6630
email—sales@dayone.co.uk
website—www.dayone.co.uk

The image on the cover and throughout this booklet is used
under licence from Shutterstock.com

Printed by Orchard Press Cheltenham Ltd

CONTENTS

ACKNOWLEDGEMENTS

I would like to thank the adoptive parents, grandparents of adopted children, prospective adopters and other Christians who read and commented upon the contents of this booklet. Without their help and support it would never have reached publication. I also acknowledge the help of the former British Association for Adoption and Fostering (now part of CoramBAAF) and of Adoption UK, who do so much to support adoptive families.

INTRODUCTION

The adoption myth

Adoption is sometimes thought of as something rather wonderful and romantic. A loving family rescues a lost and lonely child. In the new family, the child will be protected and nurtured. Whatever pain or traumas the child has endured will be instantly forgotten. The child will be immediately grateful for the love and care that he or she receives and, just like in the stories we heard when we were young, everyone will live happily ever after.

This needs to be seen for what it is: a myth.

While it is a myth, it can be seductive. It can be perpetuated by television sitcoms. It can be an unspoken message in children's stories and movies that portray family breakdowns as being quickly and painlessly set right. The myth is not challenged when we see posters aimed at potential adoptive parents showing children playing happily or looking adorable for the camera. It lives in the public consciousness and, like all myths, it is dangerous if it is believed.

For years now, my wife and I have listened to and read about people who have adopted children. We have discussed with them the joys and challenges that adopting children can bring. We have also talked with teachers, social workers and others who are interested in adoption. We have a special interest here: we are adoptive parents ourselves. So I have written this short booklet as someone who listens to adoptive parents and to those who work with them. I write what I have been told and what I have read and learned.

As noted above, there are many mistaken beliefs about adoption. In this short booklet I try to deal with the subject of adoption realistically. As a Christian, I want to stay in the real world, not in the realm of myth and fantasy. What I say may at times seem hard or even depressing, but it is not my intention to be a prophet of doom crying 'Woe, woe, and three times woe!' My role is as one who has something to share. I hope I can be someone who, to use the words of Paul, is 'speaking the truth in love' (Ephesians 4:15). Truth can liberate us from the burden of unrealistic expectations. Love covers a multitude of sins (1 Peter 4:8).

My interest has been in those who have adopted children from within the UK, where I live. Such adoptions are sometimes referred to as 'domestic adoptions'. Those who have adopted or who are thinking of adopting children from overseas may find parts of this booklet helpful but will probably also need to look elsewhere for the information they need.

Usually, when setting out to write a booklet like this, one of the first things an author wants the reader to know is his or her name. I have chosen to write under a pseudonym, and I hope that my readers will understand. My aim is to share what I can about adopted children and the families to which they belong. I hope that what I say will be discussed and will be helpful. I do not want to be the focus of attention. It is the message, not the messenger, that is important here.

Being one who listens, I do not write as an expert. I want to come alongside as a friend and to share what I believe to be true. I would like to stimulate discussion among friends, in families and in churches. If what I have written is found to be helpful, I will be pleased with having achieved my purpose. If not, my hope and prayer will be that someone whose knowledge and wisdom are greater than mine will be able to help where I have not.

This booklet is intended for a variety of people, including:

- Those who are thinking of adopting children;

- People whose friends, relatives or fellow church members may be thinking of adopting a child or children;

- Those who have recently adopted a child or children;

- People who know an adoptive family;

- Those who have an adopted child in their church or extended family;

- All those who want to know about adoption.

My experience of adoption was gained in England. I hope, however, that most of what I have written will be applicable to people in the rest of the UK and beyond. Laws and systems may vary from one country to another, but human needs, the effects of sin and the grace of God are universal.

Why is there a need for adoption?

I do not believe that adoption was part of God's original plan for humanity. The sad fact is—as we are reminded by the title of the series of booklets to which this one belongs—we live in a fallen world. Things are not as they should be. Sometimes we just have to do the best we can in the situations in which we find ourselves.

For example, many of us believe that God did not intend us to be violent towards each other, but if a woman is attacked by a man intent on rape, does she have the right to defend herself? I think the vast majority of us, whether we are Christians or not, would say that she does. If she does use violence to fend off the attacker, she is doing something which is not part of God's original plan. It is, however, morally justifiable, given the circumstances. Put simply, it may be the best option she has.

Similarly, I would say that God did not intend children to be brought up by anyone other than their parents and birth family. In a fallen world, however, this is not always possible. Some parents die while their children are still young. Others have mental health problems, are physically or sexually abusive, have alcohol or other drug problems or have severe learning difficulties. For these and any number of other reasons, some children cannot grow up with their birth parents. In these situations, we have a moral responsibility to do the best we can, even if we can no longer do what God originally intended. In some cases, but certainly by no means all, adoption outside of the family can be the best and most viable option.

Why do people volunteer to adopt?

The desire for a child

One of the most obvious reasons for adoption is the desire for a child. This is a natural, God-given urge. Men and women both feel it, whether they are married or single. I suspect that it is something that most of us can understand. If you have tried to have your own child and have been unable to do so, it is something you may know in a very real and painful way. You may also have experienced the reactions of others, both helpful and unhelpful, to your situation. However, it should not be assumed that this is the reason why people want to adopt children.

To give a child a home

Another common reason is to give children a place to live and people to care for them. Every child needs a home of his or her own. We all need somewhere to 'belong'. We all need people to call our own, and this is especially true for children.

Social responsibility

Some adoptive parents are motivated by a desire to make the world a better place or to be a good citizen. If we are going to address the many problems our communities face, we need to start with our children. We have to give them the best start in life we can. What they do with that start will be up to them, but if we fail to do our best here, we will surely face the consequences. As one adoptive mother put it to me, 'I cannot be an aid worker or a mission worker, I cannot heal terrible diseases, but I can take in children who need a home. I believe I am doing my bit to make the world a better place.' For some people, being an adoptive parent is part of being a good citizen who does something good for the world.

The biblical call for justice

For Christians, another reason to consider adopting is the biblical requirement for justice. As God's people, we are commanded to seek justice for the oppressed, to defend those who are weak and to speak for those who cannot speak for themselves. Prophets such as Amos called for justice for those who needed it. If we are truly to behave as God's people, we must do the same. Obedience to a biblical command can prove costly, as both the Bible and church history show. A command, however, is simply what it is: a command. It is not an option. Adopting a child can be one way in which Christians obey the biblical call.

The Christian's attitude to adoption

So what attitude should Christians take towards adoption? As stated above, while I do not believe that adoption is what God originally intended, in many situations it can be the best option we have. For the adoptive parents, it can fill a deep-felt personal desire. More importantly, it can provide a home and family for a child who is in need. It can be a way to be a good citizen and to help make the world a better place. Most importantly of all, it can be an act of obedience to the biblical requirement: our God is a God of love and justice, and if we are to follow him, we must show love to those in need. We must also seek justice, especially for those who cannot obtain it for themselves. God has adopted us into his family (Ephesians 1:5; Romans 8:23). He has loved us, so we should love others, with adoption being one possible way (among many) to show sacrificial love.

For these reasons, I believe that Christians should support adoption when it is necessary. This will involve someone, often but not always a couple, taking in a child or children who were not theirs by birth. It will also mean that the local church will have to find ways to accept and care for the new children. It is to these matters that we now turn.

Thinking of adoption

Perhaps you are thinking of adopting a child. Or perhaps you know someone who is thinking of doing so. Before you (or they) make this decision, consider this: Is your (or their) understanding of adoption realistic? Is it based on the evidence of others? Is it based on a biblical understanding of human nature and the effects of sin? Or is it based on a naïve belief that there are no serious problems to be faced and everyone will live happily ever after?

If you are considering adoption, try to talk with as many people who have adopted as possible. Listen to them and try to learn what you can. If you are a Christian, it would be good if the adopters you contacted shared your Christian faith. If they do not, you can still learn from them. Moses took advice from his father-in-law who was not a Hebrew. In school, I learned from my teachers (although some may say I didn't learn as much as I should have done!). Most of them were probably not Christians, but that does not diminish the validity of what I was taught.

It should be remembered that no two children, adopted or otherwise, are ever exactly the same. Indeed, one of the most significant issues that prospective adopters may have to face is that they simply do not know what problems their new child will have. That said, the list below shows some situations and behaviours that adoptive parents may have to address. This list is not designed to frighten or depress you (and a particular child may not have any of these behaviours), but rather to cause you to think about these issues, pray about them and discuss them with any adoptive parents you meet. Finally, ask yourself how you would cope if these situations were to occur in your family.

Trauma-triggered behaviour

Trauma-triggered behaviour occurs when something, consciously or unconsciously, reminds the child of a past traumatic event. The trigger is often something quite harmless and unintentional. It can, however, result in the child being extremely distressed, often crying or screaming uncontrollably.

Good behaviour in public but difficult at home

Some adopted children are fearful of misbehaving in public and so will appear to be very well-behaved at school, at church or anywhere where he or she is supervised by others. At home, however, where the fear is less, the child can be much more difficult. This can cause some people to see the adoptive parents as being in some way inadequate or as not setting enough boundaries for the child.

Relating to one parent but rejecting the other

Some children from very traumatic backgrounds can relate to only one caregiver. This can have various consequences. It can be exhausting for the parent to whom the child does relate. (Remember: this will be a very needy child.) It can also require a great deal of emotional maturity from the parent who is constantly rejected. Finally, it can lead to the rejected parent being judged by others as not being sufficiently involved with the child.

Inappropriate demonstrations of affection

As they grow older, most children learn what is, and what is not, appropriate with regard to affection and touch. However, not all children have the opportunity or the environment in which these skills can be developed. Some children who have been taken into care have not been able to develop the usual skills in this area and need help to learn them.

'Crazy' lying

We might assume that a child who has told a lie will admit the untruth if confronted with conclusive proof of what he or she has done—at least, by a certain age. This, however, is not always the case. As an adoptive parent, you may have to address what is sometimes referred to as 'crazy' lying—that is, lying in the face of incontrovertible evidence at an age when most children would have progressed past this stage.

Fear

It is sometimes assumed that children want to go out and explore the world, to face new challenges and to have adventures. A child who has suffered abuse or moved through the care system may, however, simply want to stay at home. The outside world may seem just too much to face.

Anger

Anger is often the result of fear—and adopted children, due to their backgrounds, can be very fearful. Some adopted children blame their new (adoptive) parents for breaking up their family of origin. Whatever the cause of the anger, it is not easy to live with someone who is constantly angry, even if that person is a child.

Violence

Sometimes fear and anger can result in physical violence. This can be towards the other children (either birth children or adopted) or against the parents. Coping with this, if it occurs, can be a challenge physically, emotionally and spiritually.

Urinary and/or faecal incontinence

We normally associate lack of bladder and bowel control with babies, or perhaps with the most elderly. Adopted children can, however, be emotionally disturbed and/or developmentally delayed. They can therefore need the support that we would give to a much younger child.

Self-harm

Anger is not always taken out on others. Sometimes, people who are in pain as a result of past experiences take out their feelings on themselves. The 'translation' of emotional pain into physical pain can make it easier to bear.

Inappropriate sexual behaviour

Some adopted children have not learned appropriate boundaries with regard to touching themselves or others. Language and/or behaviour can become sexualized at an inappropriately early age. For adoptive parents, responding to inappropriate sexual behaviour and teaching what is appropriate can be a challenge.

Past sexual abuse

Sadly, many children who have been placed for adoption have suffered abuse. This can include sexual abuse. This can lead to various problems for the child concerned. The adoptive parents may need to learn how to deal with this.

Persistent stealing

Property is another area in which a new child may not have learned adequate boundaries. Persistent stealing, either within the family or outside, can be a challenging issue.

Persistent refusal to go to school

Not every child likes going to school, but adoptive parents may have to cope with constant refusal to attend school as required. Helping the child to settle into a new school or finding some other way for him or her to be educated can require patience and creativity.

Lack of comprehension of another person's pain or distress

Some adopted children find it very difficult to understand another person's distress. It would be wrong to see the child as being cruel, as he or she simply does not understand what is happening. Helping a child to understand the feelings of others can take time and effort.

Lack of response to the usual methods of reward and punishment

The shelves of both Christian and secular bookshops usually offer plenty of choice when it comes to books about how to bring up children. Added to this is the advice we may receive in sermons or from well-meaning friends and relatives. Finally, there is whatever we may find via the Internet.

For some children, however, the usual methods of child-rearing are unsuccessful or even counter-productive. Finding methods that do work for your child can be a challenge.

More than one adopted child

Many people who adopt children come from families where they had brothers or sisters, or both. It is normal to want this for our own children, even if we did not have it ourselves. In a family of birth children, this can result in a certain amount of rivalry as different children compete for the parents' attention. Adopted children, however, have often been deprived of parental attention and can therefore crave it all the more. As a result, the normal rivalry that exists between siblings can be far more extreme.

People who adopt a sibling group will experience an exponential increase in the number of relationships within their household. For example, a couple without children have only one relationship in the house. If a child is born or adopted into the family, there are three relationships to consider. A couple who adopt two children at once will immediately have six relationships to manage and maintain.

Birth children still at home

Some adoptive parents have birth children who are still living in the family home. This can result in problems with regard to the amount of attention that each child receives. Sometimes, birth children and their new adopted siblings like each other—but sometimes they don't.

It is important to note that none of the above is a reflection on the adopted children themselves. All children, adopted or not, are made in the image of God. They, like all of us, learn to adapt to their environment. If that environment is unpredictable or abusive in any way, the child will adapt accordingly. Then, if the environment is changed, children, like all of us, will take time to learn how to live in that new environment. Facilitating this process will require great patience on the part of adoptive parents and others. They may need to remember time and again that love is patient (1 Corinthians 13:4).

It should also be kept in mind that, while an adopted child may present with more than one of the above challenges, some adopted children may have none of them.

Questions to ask others

If you meet with other adoptive parents, you might find it helpful to ask them some of the following questions:

1. *Would those who have adopted in your area suggest applying to your own local authority or somewhere else?* Are there any local authorities or other adoption agencies near you that they would recommend or, conversely, suggest that you avoid?

2. *How much do the people at the local schools know about adopted children?* Children spend a large amount of their waking hours in school, and success or failure here will be profoundly important.

3. *Do the local schools recognize that adopted children have their own particular needs?* Adopted children are different. Treating all children the same is not always appropriate. Do the local schools recognize this? (We will look at this in more detail in Chapter 4, which includes research findings that indicate something of the extent of the problems adopted children can face in school.)

4. *Is there a school that other adopters would recommend?*

5. *If the staff at the local schools are not well trained in the needs of adopted children, are they at least willing to learn?*

6. *Will your local education authority be willing to move your child to another school, or to a special school, if you think it necessary? Will they have the funds to do so?* (If the answer to this question is 'No', you may need to ask yourself if you could cope with taking your case to a tribunal. It might in that case be helpful to talk with other parents, whether they are adoptive parents or not, who have faced the challenge and expense of a tribunal hearing.)

7. *Are the other services in your area, such as health and social work, aware of the needs of adopted children?* If an agency says, 'Our staff are very well trained,' is this consistent with what you hear from other adopters? Do these local agencies treat adoptive parents with respect and take their concerns seriously, or are they patronizing and dismissive?

Questions to ask yourself

It is important that you also think about the following questions for yourself:

1. *Have you considered your extended family?* Grandparents, uncles, aunts and cousins can be absolutely invaluable. Will they accept an adopted child as being one of their own? Will they continue

to love and accept the new member of the family, even if the child has behaviours and difficulties that those born into the family do not have? (If they will do so, thank God for them. If not, it is time for very serious thought and prayer.)

2. *Have you considered your neighbours?* Good neighbours, like a good family, can be immensely helpful. Are your neighbours willing and able to give support when needed? Would you trust them with childcare if necessary? Will they understand if your child does not always behave as he or she 'ought' to behave?

3. *Have you thought about your own stamina?* Children from severely disrupted backgrounds can absorb huge amounts of time and energy, often giving little or nothing in return. Can you cope with anger, rejection, violence or constantly being ignored? Will your relationships survive? Consider the state of your health, both physical and emotional. Think about your marriage. Think about the effects on your career. Pray for wisdom.

The adoption process

Many people are wary of the adoption process. It can take time and, understandably, there are a lot of questions asked. It is easy to feel that all the power is with those who will make the final decision about whether or not a child is placed with you. It may be useful to remember that, as a prospective adopter, you are offering the adoption authority and the community in general something very significant.[1]

If you accept a child for adoption, the authority concerned will have one fewer child in their care. You will also be saving the taxpayer a very large amount of money. This will not be without cost to you or to those around you. It is important, therefore, that you do not allow yourself or your offer to adopt a child to be undervalued.

When you are thinking of adopting, one question you will need to work through is whether you should

---

1   For a fuller discussion of the adoption process, see S. Donovan, 'Are Social Workers Being Dishonest about the Realities of Adoption?', Community Care, 16 September 2014, http://www.communitycare.co.uk/2014/09/16/ dishonesty-adoption-setting-children-families-fail/?cmpid= NLC|SCSC|SCDDB-2014-0916.

apply to your own local authority, another local authority or some other adoption service.

Applying to one's own local authority has the advantage of being closer to home and therefore more easily accessed. A disadvantage is the possibility of meeting your child's birth parents somewhere you do not expect, such as in your town or supermarket.

When you approach an adoption agency, think about the following questions:

- Do the agency staff treat potential adopters with respect?

- Does the agency appear well organized and efficient? Are messages passed on to the appropriate person? Are their answers prompt and accurate?

- What post-adoption support would they offer, and for how long?

- Do they offer an adoption allowance? (Adopting needy children can affect your ability to earn a living, so an adoption allowance may be necessary.)

- Do they have a programme of ongoing support and education for adopters?

- If you are adopting from your own local authority, are the post-adoption support staff familiar with the special educational needs services in the area? It may be useful to ask to meet some of the post-adoption staff before you decide where to adopt. Perhaps you could ask them if they know the names of those in charge of special educational needs in your area. Do they know who is responsible for children with special needs in the local schools? (In schools in England, the member of staff who is responsible for children with special educational needs is usually called the Special Educational Needs Co-ordinator, or 'SENCO'.)

- If you were to have a dispute with your child's education authority, such as over which school he or she should attend, what kind of support would they be willing to give you? Can they give you any examples of cases where they have supported the adoptive parents against the wishes of their colleagues in the education service?

Do not be afraid to ask questions. It is in the best interests of you, the child and everyone else that you have an honest and open dialogue with the adoption agency. If you have the opportunity to ask questions in person, do not be afraid to use it. Alternatively, you could ask the adoption agency for the email address of someone on their staff to whom you could submit questions.

Asking questions is not always easy. If you are someone who finds it difficult to confront others or to ask difficult questions, you may need to think about how to approach this. It might help to do some reading on assertion skills before you start the adoption process. Some people, including Christians, confuse assertion with aggression. Being assertive, however, does not mean being manipulative or aggressive. It means not being passive; saying what needs to be said while showing respect for others. Read about it, think about it, and, as with everything, pray about it.

If you decide that adoption is not for you

It may be that, after reflection, discussion and prayer, you decide that adopting children is not for you. This in itself can be a great loss. For some, it will mean accepting that they will never have children either by birth or by adoption. Although this is a loss of something that is intangible, it is still very real and the grief it causes can be significant. As with all losses in life, it is important that the resulting grief be recognized and respected.

If this is your situation, it is important that you do not feel guilty about the decision you have made. We have different gifts and talents. No ministry is any more, or any less, important than any other. If the gifts God has given you do not equip you for this particular field of service, that is his choice. It may be that part of your ministry will be to support an adoptive family, or it may not. The important thing for all of us is that we serve God using what he has graciously given us.

A new child

The rewards

There are many rewards in having children, whether by adoption or by birth. Watching as children grow to adulthood and achieve their potential is one of life's great experiences. Hearing that your child has passed an exam, reading a good school report or being present as your child performs in a school play are truly wonderful experiences to enjoy and remember. Likewise, it can be thrilling to watch a child compete, and sometimes win, at sport. When you know that your child has overcome a host of difficulties to get to that position, the experience is so much greater.

Adoptive parents can also keep in mind the fact that, without people like them, children would either remain in an unsatisfactory home environment or be left in the care of the state. Adoptive parents should also know that whatever support they receive is almost certainly outweighed by the enormous amount they have saved the taxpayer. For adoptive parents who are committed Christians, there is the knowledge that they are responding to the biblical call for love and justice. Whatever sacrifices they may have to make are being made for God. They are part of his work on earth.

The challenges

Every adopted child has special needs

It goes without saying that children who are taken into care are placed there for a reason—and that reason has to be significant. As noted earlier, it may involve abuse (physical, emotional or sexual), neglect or any number of other painful situations. Every child is different, but what is certain is that your newly arrived child will have experienced things that God did not intend and that no child should ever have to face. The very act of taking a child into the care system, while often necessary, can be a significant trauma in itself.

For this reason I do not ask, 'Does your adopted child have special needs?' Every adopted child has special needs. Saying this to others may not always be easy or popular, but it needs to be said. As Christians we are called to speak the truth in love (Ephesians 4:15).

Getting support for yourself

Being a husband, wife or parent is a role we have twenty-four hours a day, seven days a week. That is the way it should be. Being the parent of a particularly needy child can, however, be exhausting. Will you be able to get any respite? Is there someone such as a member of your extended family, a trusted friend or someone from your church who is willing and able to take care of your child occasionally? Just as important: Is there someone you can call for help if you are feeling exhausted? If you do not have outside support, do you have the strength to carry on seven days a week for years or decades?

It is important to maintain relationships with friends, family and other people you find supportive. This will take up time and may involve some planning. If you are married, you may need to ask how you will spend sufficient time with your spouse. In each case, whether with friends, family or your spouse, you need to spend time talking about yourself and the person you are with, not just about the child or children. Practising good self-care is not something we do as an alternative to caring for our children; it is something we do *so that we can* care for them. Take good care of yourself, and do not feel guilty about it.

Feeling inadequate

Caring for children is a challenge, and adopted children bring their own unique and very real challenges. As an adoptive parent, you may find that you do not always have the answers you need. It may help to know that it is not uncommon for adoptive parents to feel that they are not up to the job.

Make sure that there are people to whom you can go to get help and support at times when you may feel that you or your parenting are in any way lacking. Are there people in your life who will listen to you in a non-judgemental manner? Do the people to whom you would go know when and how to give advice and when to stay silent?

Not all adoptive parents feel that they cannot cope or that they are in any way inadequate. Nevertheless, it is wise to be prepared.

A new child in church

Our churches should be accepting places where everyone, particularly those who seem unwanted by the outside world, is welcomed and loved. Often this is the reality. We need to remember, however, that the people who make up churches are human. They have their limits just like anyone else. How will your church, especially the leaders, respond if you adopt a child or children?

Think about the following questions regarding your church leaders:

- How have the leaders in your church handled other difficult situations where people were in need of help and support?

- Did they seek to understand the problem and did they offer practical help?

- Have they been willing to learn?

- Have they treated those with problems with respect, and refrained from rushing in with their own advice?

- Have they prayed about the problems?

Let us consider some of the challenges your church might have to face:

- *The effects on the parents: they may have less time for 'church work'.* As parents of an adopted child, you may well have less time to work in your church. You may be less available to help with Sunday school, mid-week meetings and other church activities. Will your church leaders understand this? Will they see your work as an adoptive parent as part of your Christian commitment?

- *The public image of the church.* People in churches, as in schools or other institutions, can be mindful of their public image. A child whose behaviour is disruptive or difficult may not help the way the church is perceived by outsiders. Can the people in your church cope with this?

The response of those in your church

Do you get the feeling that the people in your church would really love and accept your new child? How realistic is the church's teaching about family life? Does your church recognize that every family is different and has its own particular challenges? Do the people in your church see themselves as a large extended family where all are welcome, including those who do not always behave as others think they should?

As we have seen, the behaviour of adopted children can be particularly difficult and unpredictable. How would your church respond to someone who disrupted the service or otherwise behaved inappropriately? Is the church flexible enough to make changes to accommodate a child who is fearful, aggressive or in any way disruptive?

Consider too whether those who are part of your church love and care for other people who are new to church life. How do they treat the poor, the unemployed, the homeless and those who are mentally ill? If they treat these people well, there is a good chance they will also accept you and your child. If they do accept outsiders and the unwanted, thank

God for them! If not, you may need to ask how they will cope with your new child.

How can churches help an adoptive family?

The following points may be helpful for those in churches who want to love and accept an adopted child in their midst.

We have limited resources

It is stating the obvious to say that only God is omnipotent. Nevertheless, we do need to remember this. Adoptive parenting can be challenging and exhausting. None of us can be in more than one place at a time. When life is demanding, churches can be absolutely invaluable sources of support and encouragement. Practical help such as transport and emotional support and prayer can all be part of how you help your fellow Christians who have adopted a child or children.

Try not to judge

You may or may not have had children of your own, but remember that adopted children are different. A judgemental approach may simply leave a tired parent feeling totally demoralized. What adoptive parents need more often is love, understanding and support. (Remember how Paul describes love in 1 Corinthians 13.)

Be very careful about giving advice!

It is often tempting to tell others what they should do to solve their problems, and sometimes this works. Often, however, the person giving the advice can just end up looking silly. Remember that it is probably the parent who knows the child best. Giving advice to someone who is doing a job that you have not done yourself is not usually a good idea.

Do not 'normalize' behaviour

Probably one of the best-intended but least-helpful responses to an adoptive child's problems or behaviour is to normalize it: 'All children are like that.' 'It's just what children are like.' In just a few words it negates what the parent has said and dismisses the child's problems. It is probably very well meant, but it really does not help.

Do not say, 'He or she will grow out of it'

This remark is also probably well intended, but it can be equally unhelpful. Adopted children are often delayed in their development, sometimes by years. They can also have more serious underlying problems. Assuring the parent that everything will be all right in time may sound kind. However, it can raise false hopes and stop the child from receiving the help he or she needs.

Asking the family to come for a meal may not help

Many adoptive parents find the stress of taking their child or children out for a meal to be worse than cooking the meal themselves. If the adoptive mother is at home by herself during the day, think about asking her to join you for a cup of coffee—it could be a lot more helpful.

Ask the parents how you can be of help

Often in life, if we are really going to help people, we have to start by listening to them. Asking relevant questions can also be useful. For example, what would the parents like you to do if their child disrupts the worship in church? Would it help if you took the child out of the service for a while so that the parent and others can concentrate? Would it help if you sat with the family, or if the child were to sit with you?

Please do not assume that, just because the family does not mention specific problems, none exist. If the family with the adopted child start missing services, please do not assume that they have lost interest in church. Instead, go to the family and ask how they are. Try to listen and be non-judgemental in your approach.

Fellow Christians can pray. We must not be sentimental about this. We are in a spiritual battle.

The 'adoption myth' mentioned at the start of this booklet would lead us to believe that life is easy and has no real problems. Christians know that this is not so. Life in a fallen world involves struggle. There is pain and there is hardship. If we are going to serve God as we should, we will need his help; therefore always pray.

Remember that adopted children can do great things

Moses, Samuel and Esther were all adopted. They are surely three of the greatest names in the Bible. None of them were perfect, but God used all three to accomplish things that no one could have imagined when they were young. So it can be with the adopted children in your church.

The child and the wider community

School

Adoption UK is a large and very active organization that supports adoptive families. In 2014 they surveyed their members with regard to their children's experiences in school. The results provided by the 1,500 adoptive parents who responded are illuminating and at times disturbing. In their report, Adoption UK noted,

> The ability to manage both academically and socially is crucial to succeeding in school. 71 per cent of parents surveyed said their child's experience of neglect and or abuse in their early life has impacted their ability to cope in school academically and three quarters (75 per cent) said it has an impact on their child's social ability in school.

Due to the lasting impact of early life experiences *80 per cent of adopters said their child needs more support than their peers and nearly two thirds of parents (59 per cent) said their child is always trying to catch up in school and make up for their early life experiences.*

Adoption alone will not always enable a child to overcome their difficult start in life, and many children will require ongoing additional support. However, the idea that adoption alone will transform a child's life persists, with more than 3 in 4 parents telling us that some people expect their child to do well in school because they are now in a stable, loving family [italics original].[2]

It seems clear from results such as these that choosing the best school for your adopted child is an important matter. It is probably best to visit a number of schools and also to talk to other adoptive parents in your area. The following are some questions you could ask or find answers to:

---

2 'Adopted Children's Experiences of School—The Results Are In—Research Findings April 2014', Adoption UK, http://www.adoptionuk.org/schoolresearchfindings.

- Does the head teacher listen to the concerns of parents?

- Will your child be understood? Do the staff at this school recognize that adopted children have their own particular needs? For example, will they, if necessary, allow your child to start school gradually so that he or she can get used to a new home environment before taking on full-time education?

- When you meet the head teacher or other staff, do they engage in meaningful discussion about adopted children? Do they appear interested in what you say? Do they ask questions about your child and about adopted children in general?

- If the staff do not understand the needs of an adopted child, are they willing to learn? Not every school or member of staff will be familiar with the particular challenges that adopted children can bring. Do they ask relevant questions and take note of your answers? Do they appear willing to learn from other agencies in regard to adoption?

- If you know of any other needs that your child may have (such as attachment disorder, an autistic spectrum disorder, ADHD, learning difficulties or help after experiencing some form of abuse), are these understood by the school staff? For example, what response do you get if you use a term like 'attachment disorder' to a school's head teacher?

- What is the school's policy regarding children with special needs? What is the head teacher's approach to special needs? Is it a collaborative approach, taking on the expertise of parents and other professionals? Is it the policy of the head teacher to treat children with special needs differently according to the needs of each child, or is it policy simply to treat everyone the same? (If it is the latter, look for another school if you can.)

- Does the school have someone in charge of special needs? Does the school have a specific member of staff designated to care for children with special needs (that is, a SENCO or equivalent)? If so, has this member of staff done any specific training with regard to the needs of adopted children? How easy is it to get to see this person? Is he or she someone with whom you can speak openly and who listens to your concerns?

- Is the school in the habit of asking children to draw pictures of their families or write about them? Such a task can be very confusing and distressing for adopted children.

Other possible issues for adoptive parents

It is only right that in the adoption process the needs of the child are considered to be paramount. We must recognize, however, that parents also have needs. These needs should not be seen as being in competition with those of the child. They must be considered together and be seen as complementary. A parent who does not take care of him- or herself will not be in a good position to care for a child.

Dealing with the assumptions of others

IF MY CHILD HAS LEARNING DIFFICULTIES, WILL I BE THOUGHT OF AS BEING SIMILAR?

Some—although by no means all—adopted children have learning difficulties. In such a case, it is worth asking yourself how you would cope if others assumed you had similar problems yourself.

IF MY CHILD HAS SPECIAL NEEDS, WILL I BE TREATED WITH RESPECT?

Many teachers, health staff and other professionals treat adoptive parents with dignity and respect. Sadly, however, others do not. Consider how you would respond in the following hypothetical situation.

You have thoroughly researched your son's background, diagnoses and needs. You know from your own experience and from the experiences of others that he does not always respond in the same way as other children his age. You want his time at school to be as positive and productive as possible, but you know that, for this to happen, people will need to be made aware of his past. You visit the school that your son is to attend and explain how he came to be with you, his needs and his diagnoses. Agreement is reached on how he can best be helped. All seems well.

When you arrive at your son's new school on his first day, you find that he has a new teacher whom you have not met before. The information about your son has not been passed on to her. She is totally unaware that your child is adopted or has any form of special need. You therefore begin to explain his traumatic background, the way he may react in certain situations and the best way to help and support him. However, before you have finished, you are met with a condescending smile and are told, 'Oh, there's no need to worry about it! Teachers know what to do!'

In order to deal with cases such as this, it can be helpful to have a firm but polite response prepared beforehand. (Again, it may help to have learned how to put your point across in a firm but courteous manner.) You will need also and most importantly to heed the words of Christ and pray for those concerned.

HOW SHOULD WE EXPLAIN THE FACT THAT WE RECEIVE AN ADOPTION ALLOWANCE?

The majority of people respond positively when they are told that children have been adopted. Most people see an adoption allowance for what it is: a necessary payment for those who need it. Sadly, not everyone understands this. If you do need to explain why you receive an allowance for adopting, the following guidelines may help:

- Be as calm and as gracious as you can. (Ask for God's help with this.)

- If possible, point out that adoption is primarily about giving the child a safe, secure and loving environment. (If your aim is to make money, there are many, much easier ways to do it than by being an adoptive parent!)

- Explain that adoption is a far cheaper option for the taxpayer than keeping the child in care. As an adoptive parent, you are actually saving the taxpayer a lot of money, even if you are receiving an adoption allowance. (If it were not for adoptive parents, either taxation would have to rise or government services would need to be reduced.)

- It may help to point out that adoptive parents often have to reduce their working hours in order to give their children the time that they require. This can have an effect on the family's income that makes an adoption allowance a necessity.

Situations we would rather not face

What should parents do if, having exhausted all other means, they still find their son or daughter suffering in a school where their needs are not being met? Clearly, if they are Christians, they should pray and ask for the support of their church, but what else should they do? Should they try to change the system?

When faced with this question, Christians usually turn to Paul's admonition in Romans 13 that we should be subject to the earthly authorities and therefore obey the law of the land. Fortunately, in Western democracies such as the UK and the USA, we have the means, and some might say the duty, to challenge laws that need changing without breaking them. If adoptive parents are truly to stand up for those like their children who are in need, they may at times need to be like the Old Testament prophets calling for justice for the oppressed, even if what they say is unpopular.

SHOULD I CONSIDER TAKING MY CHILD'S CASE TO THE PRESS?

This is perhaps an easier question. Countries such as the UK and the USA are blessed with a free press. It is worth remembering that this freedom was not won lightly and, despite all its faults and shortcomings, a free press is something for which we should always be grateful. If Christian parents find that they are not getting the cooperation they need from an education authority or other public body, should they take their case to the press?

If you are considering this, you may need to think about what effects this may have on your child, especially if he or she is capable of accessing newspapers or other media for him- or herself. Could your action lead to your child being bullied in school or elsewhere? Consider also the effect it might have on your ongoing relationship with the staff of the authority concerned.

That said, some parents who have threatened to go to the press have reported that the authorities they were dealing with became more helpful and their child received the help he or she needed. That can be very satisfying. However, we should not make empty threats. If you are thinking of this as an option, it is probably worthwhile to have some idea which paper or other press outlet you would approach. Have a clear idea of what you would say and an equally clear idea of what you want the authority concerned to do.

Taking your case to the press may appear to be extreme, but it is a right that we have. In all sincerity, I thank God that we have it.

SHOULD AN ADOPTIVE PARENT EVER BE ANGRY?

All this talk of the law and our right to go to the press begs the question, Should we ever be angry? After all, they do seem to be rather angry options. There are plenty of examples in the Bible of God's people being angry for a right cause. We are, however, told that in our anger we should not sin (Ephesians 4:26). We need to heed the words of James when he tells us to pray for wisdom (James 1:5).

Are there groups in your area that can meet the needs of an adopted child?

Extra-curricular activities can broaden a child's view of life and enhance the experience of childhood. It may be worth finding out if there any groups in your area that cater specifically for children with special needs. If so, what needs do they aim to meet? Do the mainstream groups in your area have the skills and ability to accept a child who may present with needs that are different from those of other children?

I trust that this short booklet has not left you feeling depressed or overwhelmed. What I want for myself and for all of us is that we are realistic. It is here that our knowledge of God and our relationship with him can be an immeasurable support. When we look at a child, no matter how damaged or abused, we are looking at one who has been created in the image of God. This child has the potential to live for God, to serve others and to make this world a better place.

As Christians, we believe in the power of God to change both our own lives and the lives of others. Our God is almighty, all-knowing and far more merciful than any of us has yet grasped. It is to this God that we can turn in times of trial, confusion and pain. We must recognize that pain is part of the Christian experience. I believe that the great Christian saint Augustine of Hippo was right when he said, 'God had one son on earth without sin, but never one without suffering.'

At the same time, we are all fallen creatures who live in a fallen world. We are affected both by our own sinfulness and by the sins of others. None of us is perfect. Neither are the structures we create, whether their purpose is for education, health, justice or anything else. When living in this fallen world we need, as far as is possible, to be as wise as serpents while still being as innocent as doves (Matthew 10:16). This is not always easy, but it is what we are called to do.

What if the adoption goes well?

While the challenges of adopting children can be great and the sacrifices that adoptive parents make are very real, most adoptions do 'succeed' in the sense that the child is not returned to the care of the local authority. Some adopted children thrive. Some go on to do great things. (Remember the biblical examples mentioned earlier!)

What if the adoption does not go well?

Sadly, however, not all adoptions do succeed. Sometimes the pain and stress are just too much and the child, or children, are returned to the appropriate authority. If this happens, it is important to learn what we can from the experience and be willing to help others when we can. As in any area of life, if we genuinely believe that we have done something wrong, we should repent and ask forgiveness as necessary. We should, however, avoid the false guilt that comes from taking responsibility for the actions of others. Self-condemnation will not help.

Towards a Christian view of pain and suffering

The experience of adoptive parenthood can involve struggle, pain and often disappointment. There is our own pain that we may feel. There can also be the pain of others, especially our children, that we feel as if it were our own. While few, if any, of us want pain in our lives, it can make us able to help others, even if the cause of their suffering is different from ours. In this way, adoptive parents and those who take their journey with them can be of great value to the church in this and many other situations.

Where can I get further help?

Websites

Advice and useful resources can be found on the following websites:

Adoption UK: adoptionuk.org

CoramBAAF: http://corambaaf.org.uk

Home for Good: http://www.homeforgood.org.uk

Legal advice

Ask other adoptive parents about legal services in your area. Can they recommend a solicitor or law firm that specializes in working with adoptive families or families who have a child with special needs? Hopefully you will never need legal advice, but it is better to be prepared.

Support groups

As an adoptive parent, you may feel isolated. Meeting up regularly with others in a similar situation will help remind you that you are not alone. Such a group can often provide invaluable help, understanding and support. It can also be a place where information is exchanged and unbiased advice is given. Ask around to see if there is a support group for adoptive parents in your area.

If there is no group for adoptive parents in your town or suburb, perhaps you could start one. If you cannot host the group in your house, consider asking your church leaders if you can use the church hall.

Please note:

This guide is produced by Day One Publications, as part of the Living in a Fallen World series. We have sought to listen to the views of adoptive parents and others and to give you an insight into the experience of adoptive families. Please note, however, that we are not qualified professionals in this field, and whilst we share the information in good faith, we cannot accept any responsibility for any claim, loss or damage resulting from following the suggestions in this booklet.

Booklets in the *Help!* series include …

HELP! How Can I Ever Forgive? (PAUL WILLIAMS)
ISBN 978-1-84625-527-4

HELP! I Can't Forgive (JIM NEWCOMER)
ISBN 978-1-84625-325-6

HELP! I Can't Handle All These Trials (JOEL JAMES)
ISBN 978-1-84625-324-9

HELP! I Can't Submit to My Husband (GLENDA HOTTON)
ISBN 978-1-84625-321-8

HELP! I Feel Ashamed (SUE NICEWANDER)
ISBN 978-1-84625-320-1

HELP! I Have Breast Cancer (BRENDA FRIELDS)
ISBN 978-1-84625-216-7

HELP! I'm Confused about Credit and Debt (MARTIN SWEET)
ISBN 978-1-84625-526-7

HELP! I'm Living with Terminal Illness (REGGIE WEEMS)
ISBN 978-1-84625-319-5

HELP! I've Been Deployed (RODDY MACLEOD)
ISBN 978-1-84625-459-8

HELP! I've Been Diagnosed with Multiple Sclerosis (JO JOHNSON)
ISBN 978-1-84625-525-0

HELP! My Baby Has Died (REGGIE WEEMS)
ISBN 978-1-84625-215-0

HELP! My Toddler Rules the House (PAUL AND KAREN TAUTGES)
ISBN 978-1-84625-221-1

HELP! She's Struggling with Pornography (RACHEL COYLE)
ISBN 978-1-84625-246-4

HELP! Someone I Love Has Alzheimer's (DEBORAH HOWARD)
ISBN 978-1-84625-323-2

HELP! Someone I Love Has Been Abused (JIM NEWHEISER)
ISBN 978-1-84625-222-8

HELP! Someone I Love Has Cancer (DEBORAH HOWARD)
ISBN 978-1-84625-217-4

HELP! Someone I Love Has Dementia (JO JOHNSON)
ISBN 978-1-84625-458-1

HELP! Someone I Love Has Depression (JIM WINTER)
ISBN 978-1-84625-460-4